Piano Technic BOOK 1

Frances Clark ® LIBRARY FOR PIANO STUDENS

Studies by Marion McArtor

Commissioned and edited by Frances Clark and Louise Goss

© 1954 by Summy-Birchard Music
division of Summy-Birchard Inc.
Exclusive Print Rights Administered by Alfred Music
All Rights Reserved   Produced in U.S.A.

ISBN-10: 0-87487-131-X
ISBN-13: 978-0-87487-131-9

Any duplication, adaptation or arrangement of the compositions
contained in this collection requires the written consent of the Publisher.
No part of this book may be photocopied or reproduced in any way without permission.
Unauthorized uses are an infringement of the U.S. Copyright Act and are punishable by law.

PREFACE

The six volumes of the PIANO TECHNIC series are designed as technical preparation for the piano literature which the student plays at each of the corresponding levels.

Of course, no book can teach technic. But a book *can* organize the presentation of technic into a logical and concise order of development.

As you study the table of contents you will see that the organization is in chapters, each chapter devoted to one of the basic positions which the hand takes as it plays any piece of music.

As you study the etudes themselves you will see that:

1. Every etude rehearses a specific technical point.

2. The technical point occurs over and over throughout the piece.

3. There is always as much experience for the left hand as for the right hand.

4. There is equal experience for all ten fingers.

5. The technical practice is done in a musical context, not in finger exercises.

Our aim is to provide musical situations so appealing that they will encourage the student to do concentrated and repeated technical practice. This is the purpose of the PIANO TECHNIC series.

FRANCES CLARK

TABLE OF CONTENTS
(Based on Positions of the Hand)

I. *Five-finger position*

II. *Five-finger position extended (sixths)*

C. Melody and Accompaniment

III. *Five-finger position contracted (chromatics)*

A. Building the Position

B. Combining Contracted Five-Finger Position with Five-Finger Position

IV. *Crossings*

A. Crossing Over the Thumb

B. Sliding the Thumb Under

C. Shifts

D. Scale Pieces

V. *Chords and broken chords*

I. *Five-finger position*

The Clock Strikes Twelve

C-G March

In march time

2.

Peasant Dance

Slow Waltz

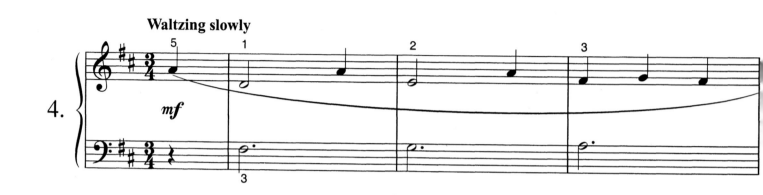

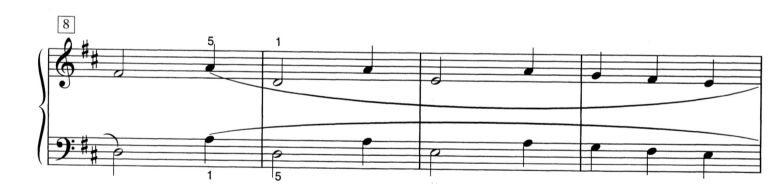

Conversation Piece

Arabian Dancer

The Bell Tolls

Lullaby for a Papoose

Bagpiper's Tune

Bagpiper's March

Folk Dance

0131

Playing Tag

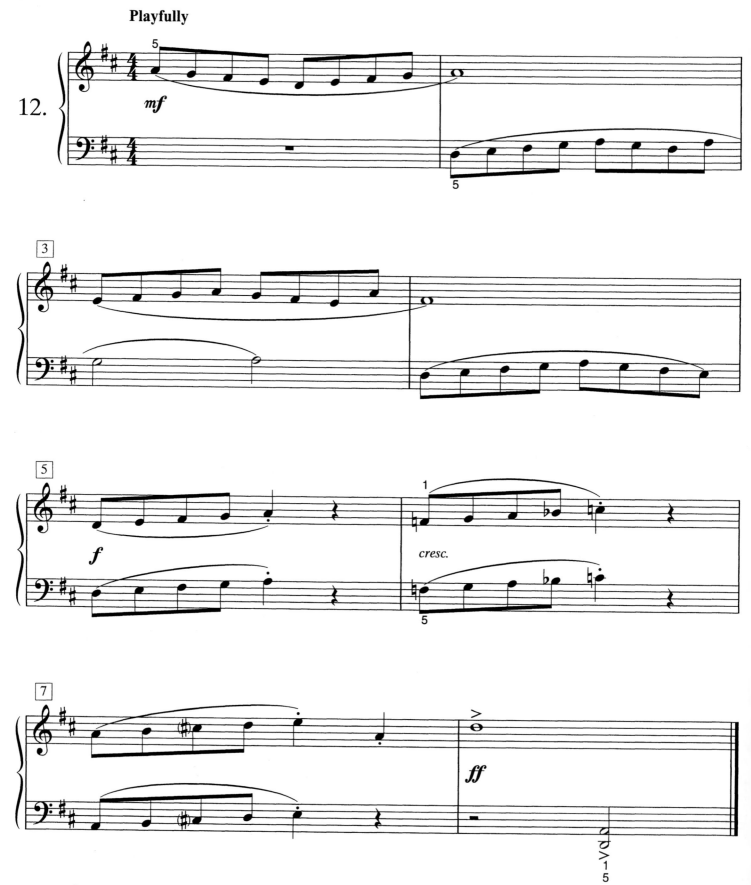

The Old Mill Wheel

Children's Parade

Elephant's Walk

18

Country Jig

Repeat Performance

Black and White

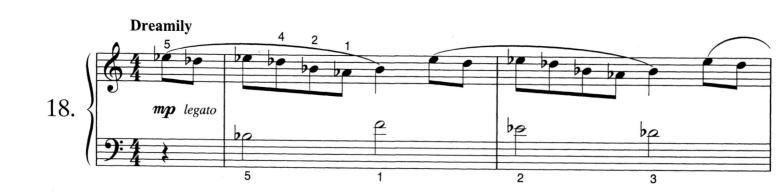

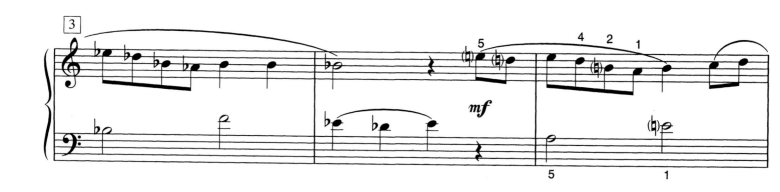

Morning Song

Evening Song

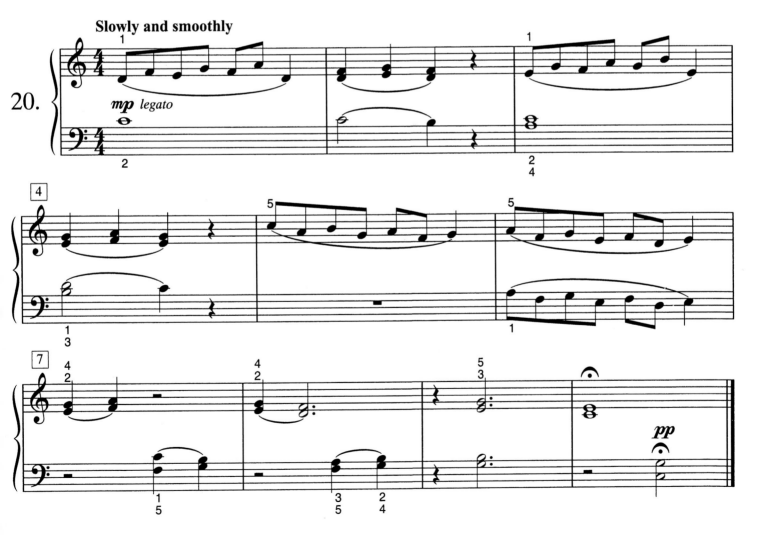

Forty Yard Dash

Relay Race

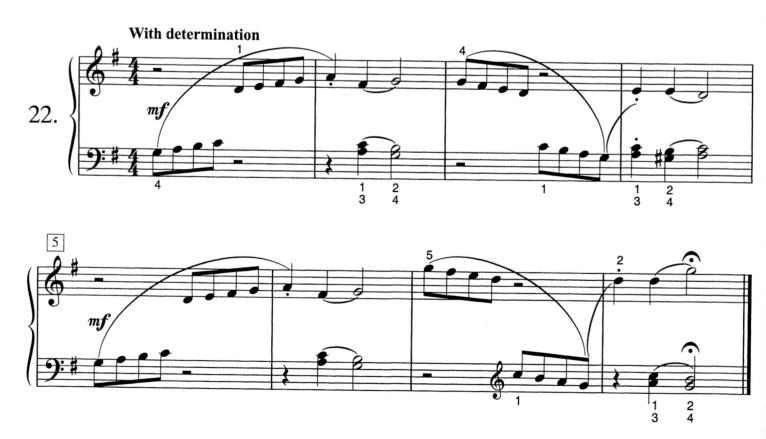

II. *Five-finger position extended (sixths)*

The Broad Jump

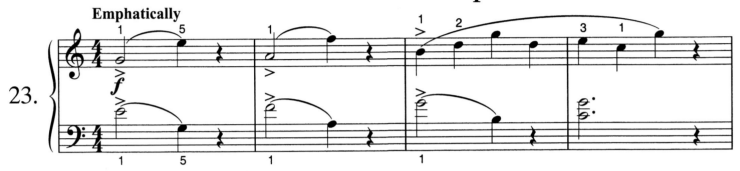

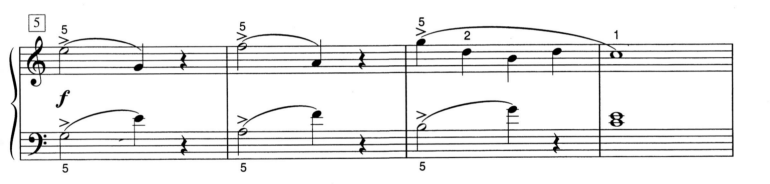

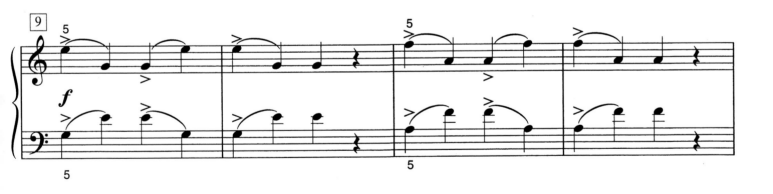

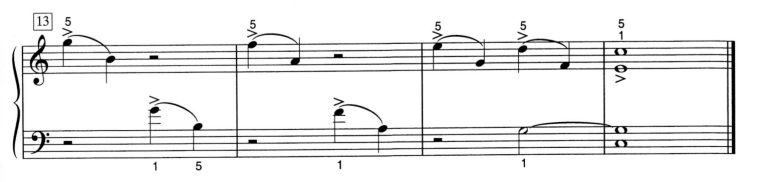

Trapeze Artists

Twin Motors

Blues Etude

Whirligig

With motion

27.

Upstairs on Tiptoe

At the Ballet

A Little Song

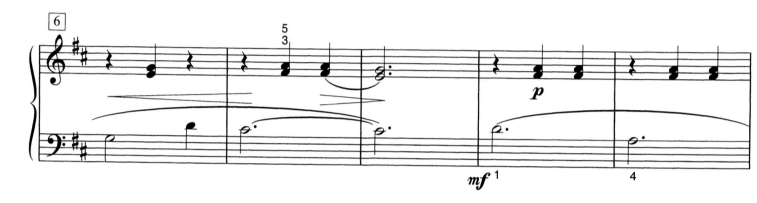

The Dancing Lesson

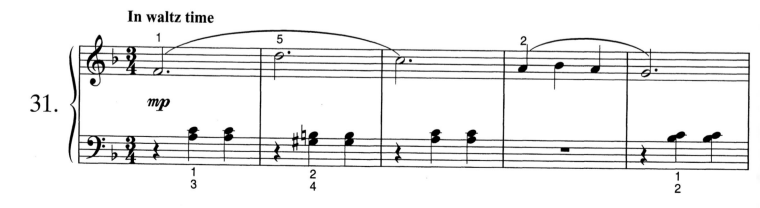

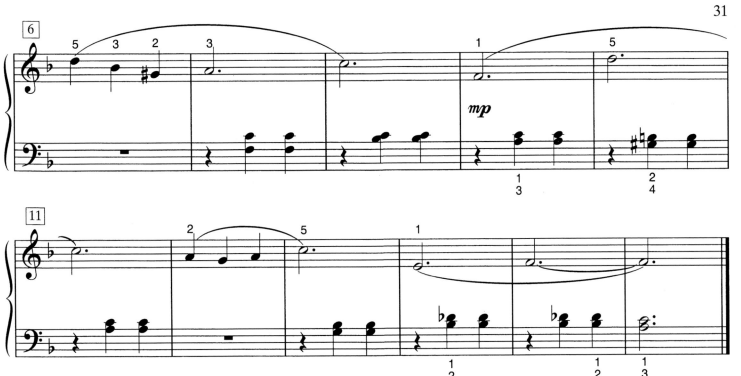

Fireside Story

III. *Five-finger position contracted (chromatics)*

Chromatic Return

Duet for Two Bees

34

Chromatic Polka

0131

Wrong-Note Blues

Unhurried

IV. *Crossings*

Skeleton Scale in C

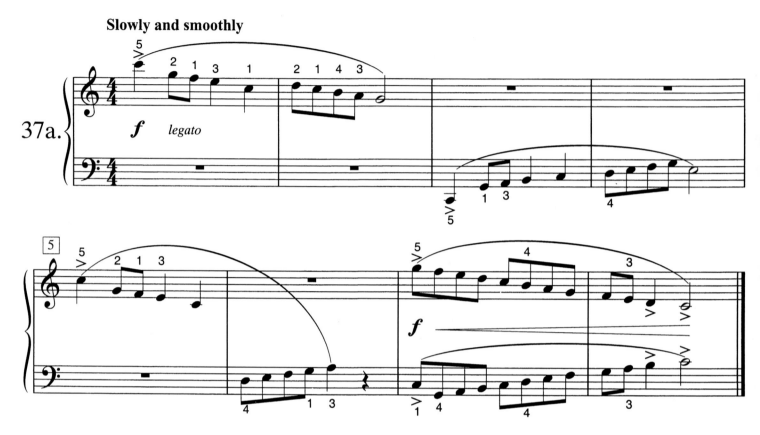

Skeleton Scale in G

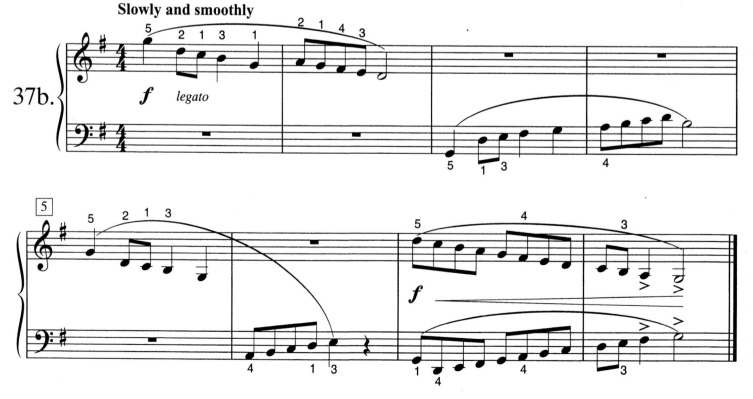

Smooth Crossing

Skeleton Scale in D

39a.

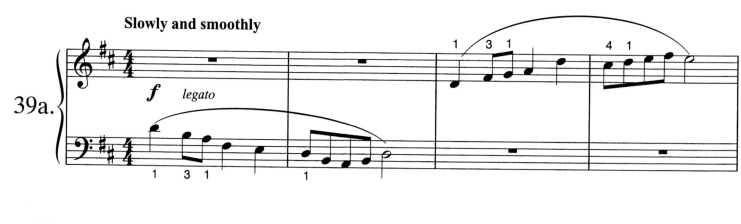

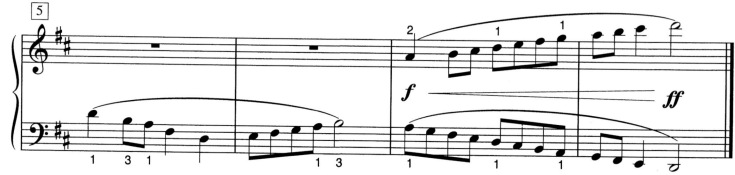

Skeleton Scale in A

39b.

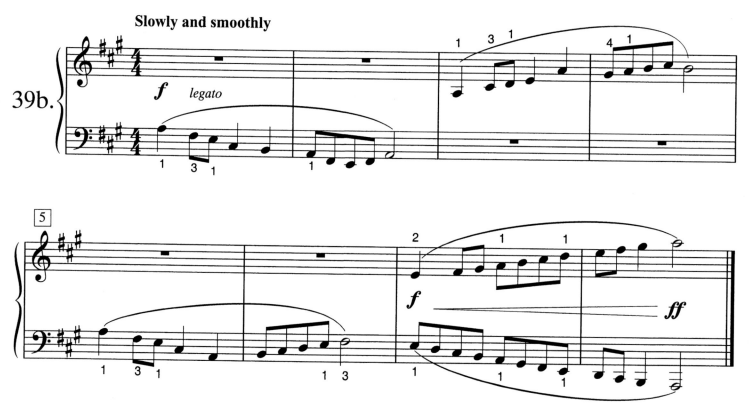

Smooth Sliding

Smoothly, with motion

Shifting Clouds

Scale Piece in C

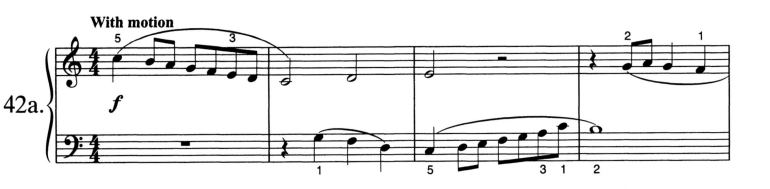

Scale Piece in D

A Sailor's Life

V. *Chords and broken chords*

Soaring

44.

A Little Memory

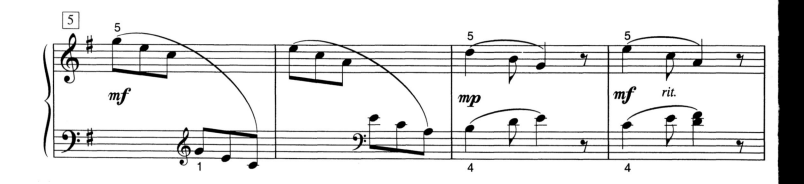

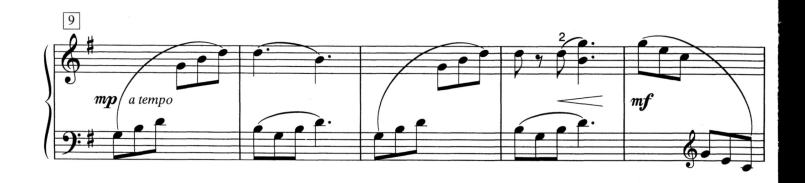

Drum and Bugle Corps

The Cadets

With military precision

47.

Elves and Gnomes

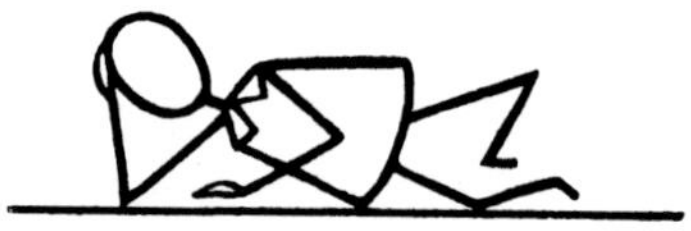